ANOTHER GOOD BOOK

Since the beginning of mankind, more thought has gone into the understanding of God than any other subject under the sun – and still nobody is any the wiser. In the length of a taxi ride, this little book explains once and for all.

GOD EXPLAINED IN A TAXI RIDE.
Paul Arden

IF YOU'RE IN A

SKIP TO PAGE

IF YOU'VE TIME,

AND ENJOY THE

BIG HURRY,
96.
SIT BACK
RIDE.

GOD EXPLAINED
IN A TAXI RIDE.

Paul Arden

Illustrations by Mark Buckingham

DIS-CONTENTS

WHERE TO?

There aren't many people who go through life without wondering what it is all about.

The world's smartest thinkers have mulled it over time and time again.

Billions of words in millions of books have been written on this subject, and yet no one is any closer to an answer.

It's about time a less wordy version was made available, a book on God that you can read in the length of a taxi ride.

THE METER'S RUNNING

Darwin says there is no such thing as God.

There is only science and evolution.

That is too stark for most of us. We need a soulmate: we gaze upwards to find him.

Most of us need something spiritual to believe in. Man cannot live on bread alone.

That is the nub of this book.

I DUNNO

Because we don't know what life is all about, we spend a great deal of time seeking answers.

There are no answers. We will never find them.

God in his infinite wisdom has made it that way, so that life becomes infinitely interesting.

It's the unknown that makes life so rich.

WHAT'S GOING ON?

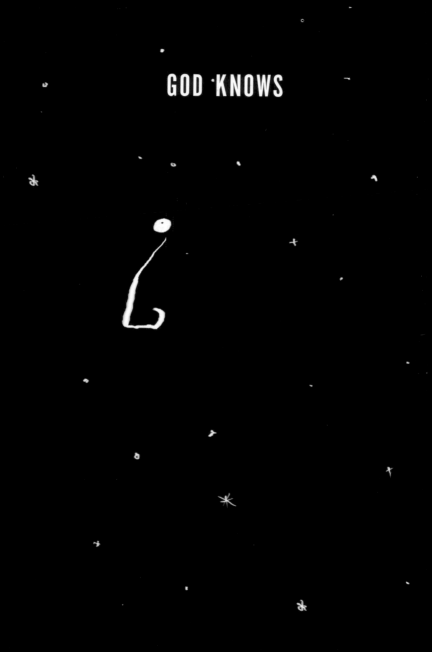

GOD ·KNOWS

SO HELP ME GOD!

When things go wrong in normal life, we get by with a little help from our friends.

When we need help that our friends cannot provide, we seek consolation in an idea and the name we give to that idea is God.

More tea, vicar?

CUTTING OUT THE MIDDLE MAN

We all have our own direct line to God.

We don't need preachers or prophets.

We just have to believe that a power or force exists that is in itself perfect.

But not many people will accept this.

It's too simple. We have to make things complicated.

And heaven knows, does the Church ever make things complicated!

WHEN THINGS GO WRONG

When things don't work out the way we want them to, we maintain our faith by shrugging our shoulders and saying . . .

'God works in mysterious ways.'

God on his way to work

YOU DON'T NEED A RELIGION

In the book *Life of Pi*, a young Indian boy comes across three good men. Each has a different faith.

Each in turn explains their religion to him.

All are equally valid, and he doesn't know which to choose.

So he doesn't choose.

THE TRINITY

When I was young, I went to church every Sunday, and the rector spoke of the Trinity: God the Father, the Son and the Holy Ghost.

The reverend never explained these things; they were read out and we would join in parrot-fashion, not knowing what we were talking about.

Nevertheless, I accepted these things in the name of God.

I am certainly not the only person to have puzzled over this conundrum.

So I thought I would make a stab at understanding it.

The Father

The Son

The Holy Ghost

SO WHO OR WHAT IS GOD THE FATHER?

No one has ever seen him.

Maybe he doesn't exist.

If he didn't exist, man would have to invent him.

WHAT IS THE HOLY GHOST?

There is no explanation for what is the Holy Ghost.

Maybe that's because nobody understands.

WHO IS THE SON?

Jesus actually existed.

His life has been recorded, glorified and dramatized.

From what we read in the Bible, he was an intelligent and charismatic man who could pull a crowd.

Like Gandhi, Martin Luther King and Nelson Mandela, he was a pacifist, and, from what we know, a good man, who gave his life for his people.

His story has been told and retold so many times that it is difficult to separate fact from fiction.

IT AIN'T NECESSARILY SO

I'm not saying the events described in the Bible didn't happen.

Maybe they just didn't happen the way the Scriptures tell us.

The things that you're liable
To read in the Bible
Just ain't necessarily so.

Porgy and Bess, George and Ira Gershwin

Two great works of fiction?

THE GREATEST STORY EVER TOLD

The Bible is a great read, but like Chinese whispers, the truth of it has become distorted.

It's hard to tell where history stops and legend begins.

It was written long after the death of Jesus, from word of mouth and hearsay.

Translated from Hebrew into Greek and Latin, again from Latin into English, and then retranslated into what we know today as the King James Bible.

It is a book the Church wants you to believe in.

It is the Church's Bible, not God's.

MIRACLES

They are a bit of a problem, but can be explained in terms of illusions.

As today we have conjurors and illusionists who perform miracles on television, so there were clever people in Jesus's day who could magic up a few tricks.

Take walking on water.

A boardwalk just under the surface provides an excellent platform for a miracle.

When someone is a star, as Jesus was, people latch on to them: often clever people who want a bit of light to shine on them too.

Jesus had disciples and, like any star, roadies to manage his tours.

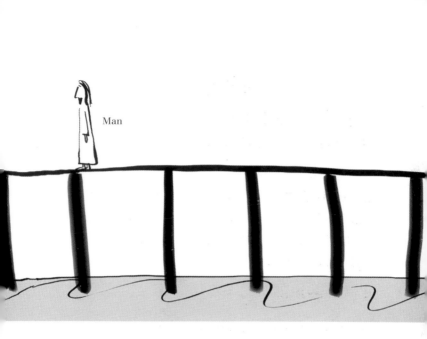

Man

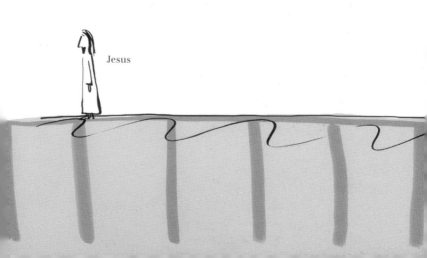

Jesus

IS THIS WHAT REALLY HAPPENED?

Christ was taken down from the cross by his friends whilst still alive.

He was then placed in a cave, and a boulder was rolled across to block the entrance. His friends attended him and tried to keep him alive.

Three days later he died.

Metaphorically this could be regarded as his ascension into heaven.

His friends rolled away the stone and buried him in an unknown location.

It's a possibility.

BLIND FAITH

How can you have blind faith in something for which there is not a scrap of evidence?

Well, the answer is you can't.

If you could prove it, it wouldn't be faith.

You can *only* have faith in what you *don't* know.

That's what faith is.

THE ANSWER IS BLOWING IN THE WIND

A young child asked his father if he could prove there is a God.

'I can't prove it,' he said.

'It's like the wind. You can feel it, but you can't see it.'

PROOF OF GOD

In the fifteenth century, St Anselm was made a saint for his proof of God's existence. It might take another taxi ride to get your head round this!

1. We define God as that for which there is no greater.

If you agree, go to point 2

2. God is perfection.

If you agree, go to point 3

3. Perfection that actually exists must be greater than merely the idea of perfection.

If you agree, go to point 4

4. Therefore God must exist: He is that for which there is no greater, and the mere idea of perfection is not as great as perfection that actually exists.

Glasgow, please?

ARE YOU BRAVE ENOUGH NOT TO BELIEVE IN GOD?

GOD HELPS THOSE WHO HELP THEMSELVES

We are God.

We are made of the same matter that makes the universe.

So when we pray, we also pray to ourselves.

It's not about prayer.

It's about wanting.

If we pray lightly and for many things, they probably won't come to us because we don't really want them.

If we pray hard and long enough for one thing, we often get what we want.

Self-service?

THE POWER OF PRAYER

GRAVEN IMAGE

Jesus is nearly always portrayed with high cheekbones and a kind expression, in a way that we would consider handsome.

That's how we see him today. It's the way he is depicted on film. Today, Johnny Depp would be cast as Jesus.

We don't know what he looked like. He could have been a little fat man squatting like the Buddha, or a bald man like Gandhi.

He might even have looked like Osama bin Laden.

SUNDAY'S THOUGHT FOR THE DAY

Hindus do not eat cows.

Anglicans eat beef on Sundays.

One man's sin is another man's roast dinner.

HEATHENS

They may have been barbaric, but they were very smart in the way they thought about religion.

They had many gods.

If they wanted rain, they prayed to the rain god and it rained, or maybe it didn't.

If they had a tummy ache, they prayed to the god of pain and if they were favoured the pain went away.

They were talking to God through things they understood.

Very simple, very truthful.

Not so heathen.

A good day for heathen prayer

AN AWKWARD PARISHIONER

The Eskimo asked the missionary, 'Will I go to heaven or hell?'

The missionary said, 'To heaven.'

'Would I go to hell if I didn't know anything about it?' asked the Eskimo.

'No,' the missionary said.

The Eskimo said, 'Why did you tell me about it then?'

Think about it.

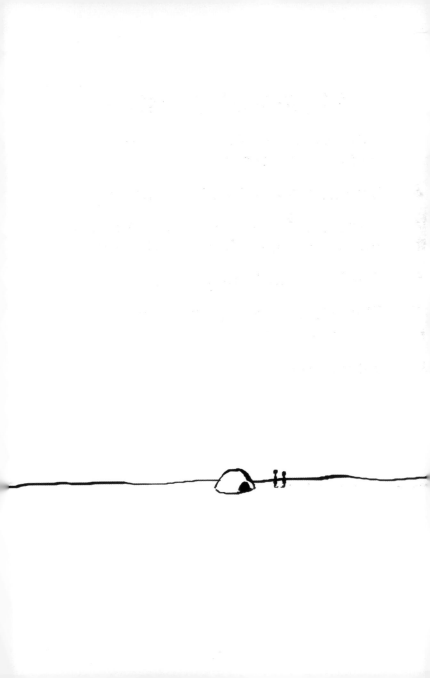

ATHEISM

Mankind does not really want to live without a God.

As the Communists have discovered, atheism is too barren an outlook to live with for very long.

Spiritually we need dear old God, but we want him on our terms, under our control.

FIGHTING TALK

You will know the story of the tower of Babel, where men were building a tower to get closer to God.

It was really built for their own self-glorification.

So God decided to restrain them by making them speak different languages.

Suddenly, they started to argue and pass judgement on each other.

The project collapsed.

Speaking different languages leads to misunderstanding, which leads to animosity, which leads to fighting.

There have been many wars in the name of religion simply because people speak different languages.

Most religions are different ways of saying the same thing. But we hear things differently because we all speak different languages.

That is why we have misunderstandings and that is why we have wars.

We fight our neighbours because we don't understand them, not because we disagree with them.

THE HISTORY OF WAR

Different people, different terrain, different weather, different food, different customs, different houses, different religions.

As man travelled more, he told others of his religion, and others told him about theirs.

That's when the problems started!

More blood has been shed over religion than any other issue.

Our refusal to understand the beliefs of others is why we continue to have religious wars to this day.

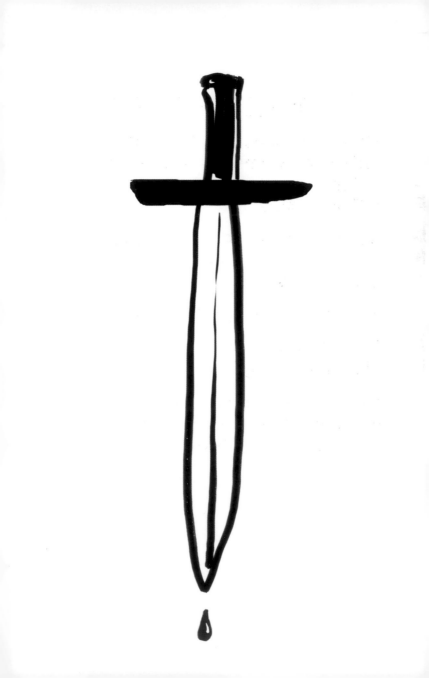

WHY DOES GOD NEED YOU TO DEFEND HIM?

It must be because you think you are more powerful than your God.

If you think your God is weaker than you, that's not much of a faith.

Does it not follow, then, that people who fight wars for religion don't have much faith?

SUICIDE BOMBERS

Young men are asked to strap bombs to their bodies to blow themselves and innocent people up.

They have been told that this will guarantee them an early place in heaven.

They are asked to undertake what the people asking them to do have not themselves done.

At least Jesus died himself.

If anyone suggests that you become a martyr, say...

'You first.'

SEND IN THE CLOWNS

Wars are started by ambitious men and women whose sense of humour plays no part in the serious business of running a country.

What if, instead of sending professional statesmen, with their self-importance and deadly seriousness, to an international war summit, we were to send some of our top humorists? Sacha Baron Cohen, Ricky Gervais, Ian Hislop and Larry David, for instance.

Can you imagine this gathering of diplomats contriving to start a war?

They wouldn't be able to, no matter how hard they tried. Their sense of humour forbids it.

When people declare war on others, they believe themselves to be just.

They believe that God is on their side.

God knows, they are insane.

Adapted from Lin Yuyang

A BUILDING FOR PEACE

If instead of showing strength by spending billions on weapons of war, the West was to build a mosque on Ground Zero, it would be a remarkable symbol of our understanding of the Islamic point of view.

It would be a major step towards world peace.

THE FEAR OF GOD

Often, ordinary people don't think they understand philosophy.

They need simple rules of life.

This is where the Church comes in.

It gets the people to observe society's rules by putting the fear of God into them.

YOU CAN BELIEVE IN GOD WITHOUT BEING RELIGIOUS

Believing in God does not make you a religious person.

It makes you a spiritual person.

A religious person is quite different.

A religious person is someone who believes in a Church, and (religiously) performs the rites and ceremonies laid down by their Church.

You can believe in God without being part of a Church.

WHY DO PEOPLE JOIN CULTS?

New religions start up daily.

Why?

Because people are endlessly looking for solutions to life's problems, and the old religions seem out of touch.

Spiritual businessmen identify these people and serve them what they are looking for. These salesmen may be charlatans but they have the charm, drive and ambition necessary to succeed.

How else would you get people to join a sect that worships a visitor from outer space or a drunken scoundrel pretending to have found scriptures written on golden plates?

This all sounds a bit far-fetched, but for many millions it seems to work.

Is this a new religion?

PAYING FOR GOD

Many religions or cults require you to pay money to their organization.

This is an important part of the hook.

If you pay for a service, you expect to get your money's worth.

If what you are getting is free, you don't make such big demands of it.

The Churches that extract the most get the most commitment.

So the more you pay, the more zealous you become.

If your local church charged a fiver* on the door, they would get a bigger and more commited congregation.

You would also get a better service!

Ten pounds at Easter and Christmas

Christian Church: the collection plate

Islam: 2.5% of your income

The Alpha Church: one month's salary

Mormon Church: 10% of your salary

Scientology: whatever they tell you to pay

MY GOODNESS

Some of the best, the nicest and most decent people I know are religious.

They are good because they spend their lives trying to be good.

A COOL RELIGION

Islamic people go to the mosque five times a day. This may seem a little over the top to a non-Muslim.

But the ritual is rooted in something very simple:

The draining heat of the sun.

Mohammed knew that for a peasant working the hot fields, prayer would be a welcome relief:

1. As a break.

2. To wash yourself, especially your feet, for cleanliness and coolness.

3. To have a drink of water (alcohol is not on the menu).

4. To have a chat.

5. To have an audience with God.

This is a civilized way for anybody to conduct their lives.

I have seen men and women in remote Turkish country villages who were beautiful, not for their physical attributes but for their serenity and glow of innocence that usually only children have.

THE CHURCH TODAY

One hundred years ago or less, people went to church, where they were told how to conduct their lives.

Today we watch television; it is our new life guru.

Where every house once had a Bible, there is now a television.

For many of us in the Western world, life is good, at least in term of basics.

We have plenty of food, money for luxuries, access to information and enough time to enjoy ourselves.

We don't feel the need for the church as a social centre anymore.

We have a new religion.

Consumerism.

Supermarkets are the new cathedrals.

I AM GOING TO DIE SOON

Until very recently, I had blind faith in a God who gave order to all things. I took a lot of comfort from that.

Recently, I had Darwin dumped on me with such clarity that it has shaken my belief to its foundations.

It's very disquieting not to believe anything.

God help me.

Charles D

THE GOD FREE CHURCH?

Atheism denies the existence of any suprahuman being. All living creatures are the result of a chance coming together of gases, liquids and solids.

According to the atheist, all notions of God are fictional. He is a mere fantasy, living far beyond the scope of rational thinking.

But isn't a firm belief in the non-existence of a God a religion in itself?

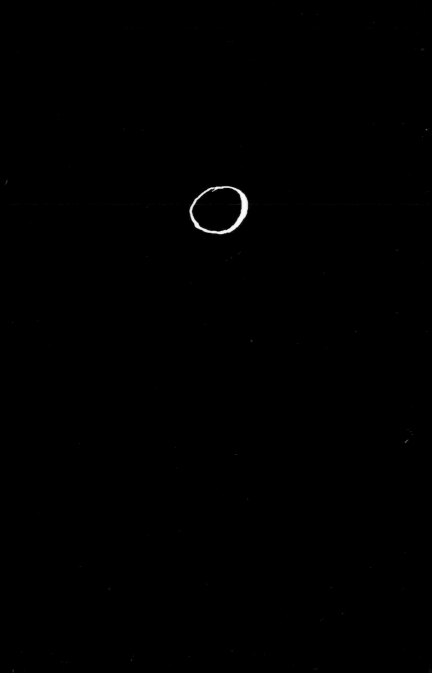

AFTER LIFE

People are scared of the dark because they don't know what's there.

As soon as they put the light on, they can see and feel safe.

We are all scared of dying, because we are afraid of the unknown.

To ease our fear of the dark, we invent explanations for the afterlife such as heaven and hell and reincarnation.

Like the light we switch on to feel safe.

IT WAS REPORTED THAT GOD SAID 'LET THERE BE LIGHT'

The sun was made by God.

Religion is a light bulb, created by man to help him to see in the dark.

An artificial light

REINCARNATION

Everyone has thoughts on what will happen when they die.

Yet no one has ever come back to tell the tale.

Some say that if you behave well in this life you get a better deal in the next.

Buddhism is based on this thinking.

It is just a guess. Nobody really knows.

Probably the most popular theory is the scientific one.

We are composed of matter, and when we die, that matter is simply rearranged in a different form.

You die.
You're buried and fertilize the plants.
The plants are eaten by snails.
Man eats the snails.
Now you are a Frenchman.

Voila!

SO, IS THER

A GOD?

AND IF THERE IS A GOD, WHERE DO YOU FIND HIM?

I FOUND HIM

HERE

↓

Petworth, West Sussex, England

WALKING WITH

AND MENTOR, I

COULD EXPLAIN

AN OLD FRIEND
ASKED HIM IF HE
GOD TO ME

LOOK, HE SAID, AT THE SUNSET. DO YOU THINK

POINTING

WHAT

MADE THAT?

DO YOU THINK ACCIDENT?

IT'S AN

DO YOU THINK
OF THE LIGHT?

IT'S A TRICK

DO YOU THINK

IT'S A FLUKE?

IF YOU DO

I BELIEVE

THEN SAY
IN FLUKES

EVOLUTION, FATE,
YOU CAN CALL IT
THEY ARE ALL
TO DESCRIBE THE

CREATION, FLUKE.
WHAT YOU LIKE.
WORDS WE USE
SAME THING . . .

THE EXISTENCE

OF GOD.

GOD IS OUR NA

FORCE BEHIND

ME FOR THE
CREATION

THAT'S WHAT

IN GOD.

BUT IF YOU DON'T BELIEVE IN GOD,
THIS IS THE END.

ACKNOWLEDGEMENTS

To my friend the Rev. Irene Arens (née von Treskow), who owns the London taxi that gave me the idea for the book.

To Christopher Macartney-Filgate, who explained God to me.

To Mark Buckingham, for collaborating with me throughout the whole process, chipping in many ideas and illustrating it in his unusual style.

To Dave Trott, who contributed three spreads to the book.

To Charlie Arden, my grandson (age fourteen), who wrote page 90, printed here verbatim.

To my daughter Harriett, who gave me the story on page 38.

To Kate Daudy, for improving my English.

To Jeffrey Windram, who I can always call on in times of desperation.

To Tony Lacey at Penguin, for once again believing in me.

To Jon Elek, for doing what great editors do.

To my wife, Toni, who I love to bits.

PENGUIN BOOKS

Published by the Penguin Group
Penguin Books Ltd, 80 Strand, London WC2R 0RL, England
Penguin Group (USA) Inc., 375 Hudson Street, New York, New York 10014, USA
Penguin Group (Canada), 90 Eglinton Avenue East, Suite 700,
Toronto, Ontario, Canada M4P 2Y3
(a division of Pearson Penguin Canada Inc.)
Penguin Ireland, 25 St Stephen's Green, Dublin 2, Ireland
(a division of Penguin Books Ltd)
Penguin Group (Australia), 250 Camberwell Road,
Camberwell, Victoria 3124, Australia (a division of Pearson Australia Group Pty Ltd)
Penguin Books India Pvt Ltd, 11 Community Centre,
Panchsheel Park, New Delhi – 110 017, India
Penguin Group (NZ), 67 Apollo Drive, Rosedale, North Shore 0632, New Zealand
(a division of Pearson New Zealand Ltd)
Penguin Books (South Africa) (Pty) Ltd, 24 Sturdee Avenue, Rosebank, Johannesburg
2196, South Africa

Penguin Books Ltd, Registered Offices: 80 Strand, London WC2R 0RL, England

www.penguin.com

First published in 2007
3

Design by Paul Arden and Mark Buckingham
Printed in Italy by Graphicom

ISBN: 978-0-141-03222-1